SPECIAL OPS

Green Berets in Action

by Marc Tyler Nobleman

Consultant: Fred Pushies
U.S. SOF Adviser

BEARPORT
PUBLISHING

New York, New York

Contents

Under Fire

Joseph Briscoe and his Green Beret team were in Iraq. Their **mission** was to stop enemy fighters from sneaking into the country.

On October 31, 2003, as the team headed back to their **base**, they heard a loud explosion. They were under attack. A **grenade** hit Joseph. He was badly hurt.

Soldiers in Iraq in 2003

The real name of the Green Berets is Special Forces. "Green Berets" is a nickname that comes from the type of hat these soldiers wear when they are not in battle.

Green Beret Charles Good came to Joseph's rescue. He tried to rush Joseph to a **medic**. As he drove, a storm of bullets stopped his **vehicle**. Charles needed to find another way out of the battle. If he didn't, Joseph might die.

Green Berets securing an area in Iraq after heavy gunfire in 2003

Road to Safety

Charles knew that there were more enemy soldiers than Green Berets. He had only seconds to figure out how to help Joseph.

As bullets whizzed by, Charles brought Joseph to the side of the road. Then he waved to an Iraqi man driving by. Was this man a friend or an enemy?

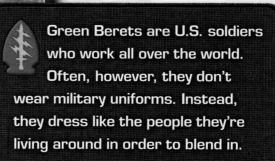

Green Berets are U.S. soldiers who work all over the world. Often, however, they don't wear military uniforms. Instead, they dress like the people they're living around in order to blend in.

Charles spoke to the driver in **Arabic**. He asked the man to take Joseph back to the base. The driver agreed. Once Joseph was on his way, Charles went back to help his team.

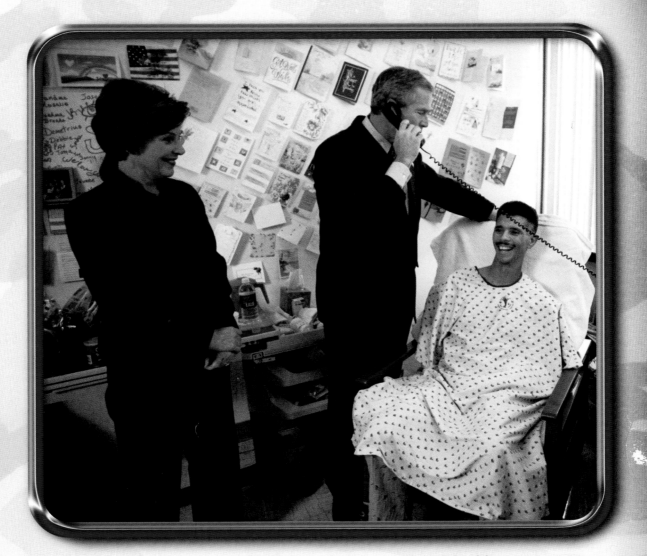

U.S. Army Sergeant Joseph Briscoe was visited by President and Mrs. Bush in his hospital room after receiving the Purple Heart for his injuries.

Risky Missions

The Green Berets are an **elite** group in the U.S. Army. They take on some of the most dangerous missions in the world. Often, they fight or spy behind **enemy lines**.

Many of their missions require them to move quickly from place to place. The work of freeing prisoners, destroying enemy weapons, and stopping **terrorists** always calls for speedy action.

Green Berets, arriving in the Philippines, on their way to a mission

Many Green Beret missions are top secret. Even the Berets' family members do not know much about their work.

While Green Berets are fighters, they're also teachers. In foreign lands, they help **locals** remove cruel rulers. They also teach others how to fight for themselves.

A Green Beret shows a soldier from Mali, a country in Western Africa, how to inspect his gun.

What Does It Take?

It is not easy to become a Green Beret. More than half the men who start the training drop out.

A trainee on a march

In order to become a Green Beret, a person must first complete the same basic training that all army soldiers go through. Next, he needs to pass a 30-day course. This includes hard **physical** tests. **Trainees** must march 150 miles (241 km) wearing 50-pound (23-kg) backpacks. They must also swim 164 feet (50 m) wearing their uniforms and boots.

After trainees pass the 30-day course, they go on to survival skills class. For 24 days they learn to live in the wild.

Trainees often have to hold heavy telephone poles over their heads for hours.

Champions in Training

After they pass the survival course, soldiers are trained to handle special weapons and give medical care. Trainees also must learn at least one foreign language. This helps them to fit in more easily while working in different countries. If Charles Good hadn't known Arabic, he couldn't have asked for help when Joseph Briscoe was hurt.

A soldier during weapons training

The last part of training is called Robin Sage. During this time, the trainees take part in real-war training. This happens over two weeks in the North Carolina woods. Other army soldiers play the enemy. Even local people get involved to make the training seem more real.

Green Beret trainees raid a prison during a Robin Sage exercise.

During the training period, soldiers also go to **parachute school**, where they practice their jumping skills.

The Team

After completing Robin Sage successfully, a soldier is awarded the Green Beret. He then joins a team of 12 men.

Green Berets in their full dress uniforms

Teams are led by a captain and an officer who is **second-in-command**. Each group has **specialists** in medicine, weapons, **communications**, and **engineering**. Some teams also have an **intelligence** specialist. These experts allow the teams to deal with almost any situation.

When on a mission in a jungle, Green Berets often cover themselves with leaves so that they can hide more easily from the enemy.

Green Beret teams have two of each kind of specialist. This means that any team can split into two smaller teams and still have all the people they need to complete a mission.

In Green We Trust

One of the main goals of the Green Berets is to earn the trust of local people. They begin by showing respect for the **culture** of the country they are in. For example, they will eat the same type of food as the locals.

Green Berets share a meal with some local Iraqis.

Green Berets also help people. In Afghanistan, they helped locals form an army, as well as build bridges and schools. They even hired locals to work at a base called Firebase Cobra. In return, the Green Berets hoped locals would help them find hidden enemies.

A Green Beret (far right) works with officers from the Afghan National Police.

Green Berets have helped new police officers in both Afghanistan and Iraq. They often teach new officers how to use weapons.

Failure or Success?

When they do fight, Green Berets are among the fiercest soldiers. In 1970, during the Vietnam War (1957–1975), they planned to crash a helicopter into a prison to rescue Americans being held there. After the crash, the Green Berets realized that the Americans had already been moved.

A Green Beret team runs toward their helicopters as they prepare for battle in Vietnam.

The Green Berets still called the mission a success. Though they had not rescued anyone, they proved that they could. The enemy now feared another **raid**. Also, knowing that the Green Berets were looking for them gave the prisoners hope. Now they knew their country was still coming to rescue them.

Green Berets searching for enemies in a jungle in Vietnam

In Florida, the military built an exact copy of the prison in Vietnam where Americans were being kept. The Green Berets used this prison to practice their rescue.

Trapped in the Desert

The military always needs information about the enemy. One night during the Gulf War (1990–1991), eight Green Berets went into the Iraqi desert. Their mission was to watch the enemy and report what they saw. They dug a hole and hid in it.

A soldier fires his weapon in the Iraqi desert.

When daylight came, they were caught by surprise. The enemy—150 soldiers—was closer than they expected. From the hole, the Green Berets fired and ducked from bullets all day.

At last, they radioed for help. Soon a U.S. plane arrived and bombed the enemy. Then a helicopter swooped down to pick up the eight Green Berets—all of them unhurt.

Green Berets are trained to survive in deserts, jungles, mountains, and icy areas. If they have to, they get by on little sleep.

Green Berets on a mission in very cold weather

Always Ready

Green Berets are always ready to fight. Yet they must be prepared for jobs that have nothing to do with battle. Jim Sissons found this out after the Gulf War.

A Green Beret talks with some Afghan children after handing out winter clothes.

The U.S. Army has one million **active** soldiers. Fewer than 10,000 of them are Green Berets.

The war left many people without homes. Fifty Green Berets, including Jim, went to a **refugee** camp in Iraq. They handed out food and water to thousands of people. The soldiers saved many lives.

Another time, Jim helped an Iraqi woman deliver a baby—in a tent! The parents named the baby after him.

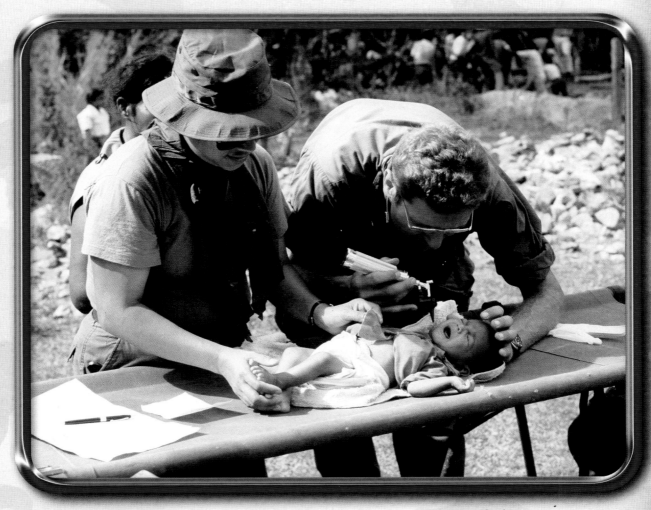

A doctor from the 7th Special Forces Group examines a baby.

Animal Rescue

Some of the lives Green Berets save are not human. For example, after the Iraq War (2003–present) began, they helped rescue a few big cats.

U.S. soldiers help carry one of the rescued lions to the Baghdad Zoo in Iraq.

While searching a palace for enemies, a Green Beret team found three lions. All were weak from hunger. So the soldiers fed them. They named the animals Xena, Heather, and Brutus. The team liked the lions so much that they soon decided to **adopt** them as **mascots**.

U.S. soldiers took good care of the lions after rescuing them.

The Green Berets even put a sign on the lions' cage that read "Special Forces' Lions. Don't mess with them!"

Red, White, Blue, and Green

Around the world, Green Berets meet people who have never traveled beyond their villages. To those people, the Green Berets are the faces of America.

Some Green Berets are teaching Afghan children how to play baseball.

While each Green Beret mission is different, the goal stays the same—to help others. Special Forces Commander Marcus Custer said, "The Green Berets like to be part of making a place secure so people have a chance for a normal life."

The Green Berets wear a patch on their uniforms that have their blood type on it. This is useful information if a soldier is ever injured and needs a blood **transfusion**.

The Green Berets' Gear

Green Berets use lots of equipment to carry out their missions. Here is some of the gear they use.

Night vision goggles allow Green Berets to see in the dark.

The **MC-5 parachute** is used by the Green Berets to jump into enemy areas.

The **inflatable boat** is light and easy to carry.

The **re-breather** allows Green Berets to breathe underwater.

The **Global Positioning System (GPS) Locator** helps Green Berets know where they are.

An **M-4 Carbine** is one of the weapons the Green Berets use.

Glossary

active (AK-tiv) when soldiers are ready to go into battle

adopt (uh-DOPT) to take in

Arabic (A-ruh-bik) a language spoken in the Middle East and North Africa

base (BAYSS) the place from which an army is controlled

communications (kuh-*myoo*-nuh-KAY-shuhns) sending and receiving information

culture (KUHL-chur) the ideas, customs, and way of life for a group of people

elite (ay-LEET) highly skilled

enemy lines (EN-uh-mee LINEZ) areas of land from where the enemy fights

engineering (*en*-juh-NIHR-ing) the science of building machines or structures

grenade (gruh-NADE) a small bomb that is thrown by hand

intelligence (in-TEL-uh-juhnss) the act of collecting information about an enemy

locals (LOH-kuhlz) people who live in a certain area

mascots (MASS-kots) animals, people, or things used as symbols for something else

medic (MED-ik) someone trained to give medical care

mission (MISH-uhn) a special job

parachute school (PAH-ruh-*shoot* SKOOL) a place where soldiers learn how to jump out of a plane or helicopter using a soft cloth attached to ropes to slow down the fall

physical (FIZ-uh-kuhl) having to do with the body

raid (RAYD) a fast, surprise attack

refugee (*ref*-yuh-JEE) a person forced to leave his or her home because of war

second-in-command (SEK-uhnd-IN-kuh-MAND) the person who is next in charge after the leader

specialists (SPESH-uh-lists) experts in particular jobs

terrorists (TER-ur-ists) groups that use violence and terror to get what they want

trainees (trane-EEZ) people who are learning how to do something by practicing

transfusion (transs-FYOO-zhuhn) blood given to a person who is injured

vehicle (VEE-uh-kuhl) a car or truck

Bibliography

McNab, Chris. *Survive in the Jungle with the Special Forces "Green Berets"* (Elite Forces Survival Guides). Broomall, PA: Mason Crest Publishers (2002).

Pushies, Fred. *U.S. Army Special Forces*. St. Paul, MN: Motorbooks (2001).

Read More

Glaser, Jason. *Green Berets*. Mankato, MN: Edge Books (2006).

Goldberg, Jan. *Green Berets: The U.S. Army Special Forces* (Inside Special Operations). New York: Rosen Publishing Group (2002).

Green, Michael, and Gladys Green. *The Green Berets at War* (On the Front Lines). Mankato, MN: Capstone (2003).

Learn More Online

To learn more about the Green Berets, visit
www.bearportpublishing.com/SpecialOps

Index

About the Author

Marc Tyler Nobleman has written more than 60 books
for young people. He writes regularly for *Nickelodeon Magazine*.
He's also a cartoonist whose work has appeared in more than
100 international publications.